Why You're the BEST TEACHER EVER!

Dear

____:

(write your teacher's name!)

You're the best! This book is full of things I think are great about you. There might also be a magical new classroom helper in here, too.

Love,

____

______________________________________,

(write your teacher's name!)

it makes me smile when you

____

______________________________________!

(thing your teacher does that makes you smile)

Here's a selfie of us:

(draw you & your teacher being awesome)

You make learning stuff . . .

- ◯ easy
- ◯ fun
- ◯ super easy & fun!

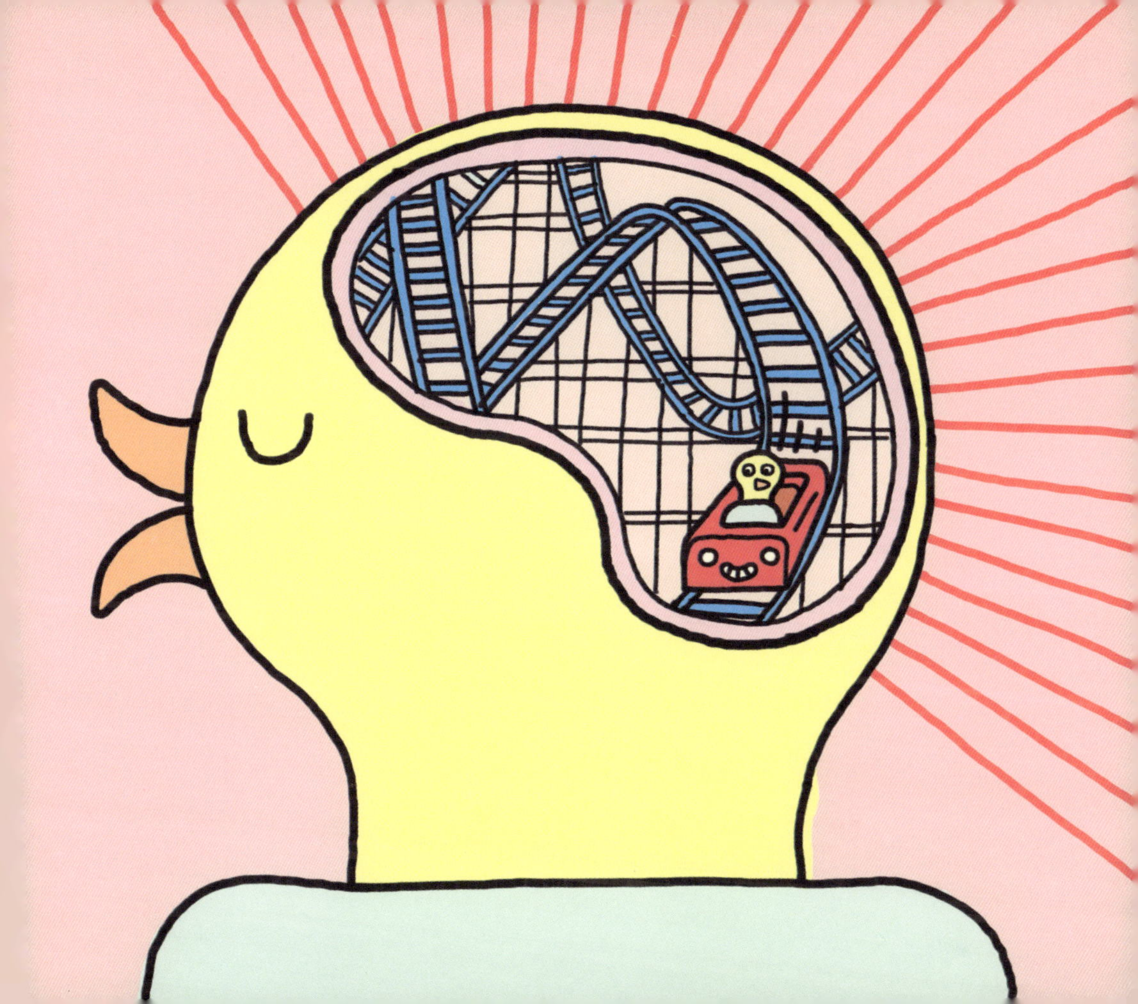

If I could, I would stay in your class
until I was

____

(write a big number here)

years old.

Awesome Teacher Math

Not Boring + Super ____________________

(awesome thing

________________________________ = YOU!

about your teacher)

I appreciate you so much!

Even more than . . .

- ○ recess
- ○ summer vacation
- ○ ____!

TRUE STORY!

______________________________________,

(write your teacher's name here)

I think you are doing a

- ○ terrific
- ○ excellent
- ○ fantastic
- ○ INCREDIBLE

job at being a teacher.

I give you

thumbs up!

(plus ______________________________ hugs)

(really big number)

If you could teach everybody,
the world would be a much

---

place!

Ta-dah!

I got you a magical classroom helper!

It's a . . .

- ○ snowy owl that makes tea & coffee!
- ○ fairy that plans lessons!
- ○ dragon that answers questions!
- ○ elf with a lifetime supply of wet wipes!

- ○ ______________________________!

(draw your teacher's new helper!)

Hi! My name is

______________ .

Did I mention, I've got free protein bars?

By the way, your student is smart and

______________ .

Also, I like your shoes!

YOUR NEW HELPER!

I am going to invent a
special teacher holiday just for YOU.

To celebrate, I will bake lots of

____

and get the whole school to dress up as

______________________________!

I like it when you say . . .

“

.”

You deserve some medals and awards!

(Obviously.)

EXCELLENCE IN THE FIELD OF

- ○ Explaining stuff
- ○ Being patient
- ○ Making jokes
- ○ ______________________________

SUPER TOP-NOTCH

- ○ Listener!
- ○ Storyteller!
- ○ Fist-bumper!
- ○ ______________________________

SCHOOL

If you were a superhero,
your superpower would be

____

____ .

Guess what? I got you a
crazy cardigan to wear to school!

Isn't it . . .

- ◯ the best sweater you've ever seen?
- ◯ colorful?
- ◯ so ugly it's FIRE?

(decorate the cardigan!)

One of my favorite times
in your class was

____

______________________________________.

(Remember that?)

I picked you some "adjective" apples!

(circle the words that describe your teacher best!)

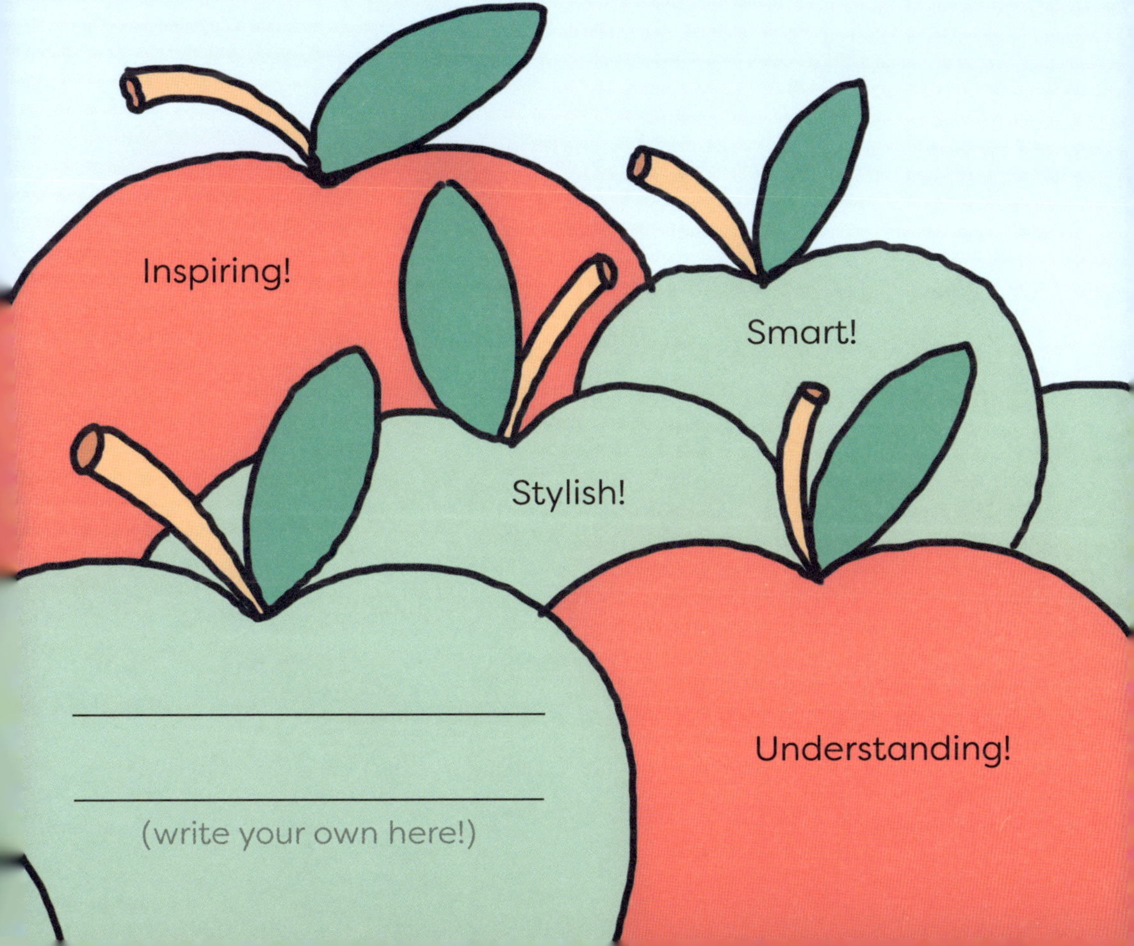
Inspiring!
Smart!
Stylish!
Understanding!
(write your own here!)

By the way, did I mention you are . . .

THE

(color in the letters!)

BEST

I really like how you
make me feel like I am . . .

(circle as many as you want!)

Important

Artistic

Good at Stuff

Safe

Special

Included

Heard

Understood

One thing you taught me
that I will always remember is

____

____.

In conclusion, I feel

____

____

that I got to learn so much from you!

THANK YOU FOR EVERYTHING!

Love,

PS: I hope you get to

____

____

this summer!

(draw a self-portrait here!)

About the Author

____

(write your name here!)

is ______________________ years old, lives in

(your age)

______________________________, and enjoys

____.

(something you like)

KNOCK KNOCK IS A REGISTERED TRADEMARK OF HACHETTE BOOK GROUP, INC.

1290 AVENUE OF THE AMERICAS, NEW YORK, NY 10104
PRINTED IN GUANGDONG, CHINA 1201-C&C-01
FABRIQUÉ EN CHINE / HECHO EN CHINA
UK DISTRIBUTION: ABRAMS & CHRONICLE BOOKS LTD.
161 165 FARRINGDON RD, LONDON EC1R

MIX
Paper | Supporting responsible forestry
FSC® C008047
www.fsc.org

ISBN: 9781683495970
UPC: 825703102420

KNOCK KNOCK® Kids
knockknockstuff.com

You Fill In The Love.®